words

in

grey

Genesis the Greykid

....

This book would not have been possible
without good friends,
good laughs, good drinks, great window seats,
rough times, happy moments,
my love for lower case letters, and people.

Special thanks to my family and friends,
but most of all, I thank my parents Russell & Angela Mcgee.
Had it not been for their continued love
through all my ups and downs,
their patience when I did not listen,
and wisdom whenever I was lost,
I don't know where I'd be.
I'll never really be able to thank you enough.
Mom, Dad, I love you.

And I can't forget to thank a super special lady,
I wrote while super far away...

(I put this letter in a bag of Hershey Kisses, sealed it, then mailed to her)

"i could of sent this in a text message,
or email perhaps.
but i wanted to translate this feeling i feel,
into the very words i wrote,
so that when you feel this letter,
in your small hands,
in some small way,
you can feel me.

to be honest....i wonder when you open this,
if your hands touched where mine laid while writ-
ing this.
when i searched in the late hours,
for words to explain the things unexplainable,
turning myself into the words,
becoming the whisper in your mind
when you decide to read this,
or perhaps...the lofty idea, of becoming the
thought
that reaches your heart,
and travels places my hands may not.
(sigh)
i know i'll see you soon...but until that day,
i'll leave you with these little kisses,
even from far away."

I've given each poem color(s) to symbolize the mood I was in during its creation. I won't tell you what the colors mean up front, just feel it out...anytime you'd like to see a brief description of what the colors mean,

flip to the back (page 77).

contents

For the last 3 years I've been conducting
poetry workshops with a crew of creatives, writers,
homeless folks, athletes (really diverse groups) in the
community.
Each session we have always consisted of exercises I'd put
together or with the help of the group collectively come up
with. The point of these exercises were intended to not only
experience something amazing together, but to also work
out different parts of the creative self.
Whether you write, draw, play sports, engineer, whatever it
is, we all felt that exercising this creative muscle in various
ways, once you applied it to your own particular craft, could
add a beautiful texture toward everything you do. With that
said, I hope you enjoy the moments you create from pages
80 onward.

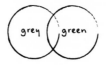

lets escape,

lets jump over the rail without looking for water,

or waste time on the debate,

the choice,

lets explore and forget our names

and find our voice under rocks that look like faces,

through the woods

leading to a farm

where simple and breathing are the same.

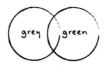

today....

on this rainy, tuesday morning,

where the fog and clouds dance,

and the wind sings its warning

of a stormy afternoon ahead,

i sit....

absolutely still,

so the clouds do not discover me -

watching from across the hill,

this rainy tuesday morning.....undress.

9

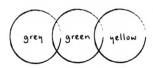

grey   green   yellow

the sky isn't,

that far away....is it?

maybe some.....visit,

can be arranged,

where its large belly that hangs,

can scrape the finger-tips...

of a boy,

who reaches for the stars.

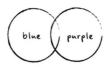

disguised as a friend,

my thoughts

waltz in,

asking if reason would like to dance,

logic....being a gentlemen,

said nothing,

and i was fooled,

again.

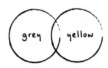

looking through this window,

at the young

and old that pass along....a song

(a tempo unfamiliar)

was caught in the wind,

blown under the door,

and into my ear

became the most favorite song,

i've already forgotten.

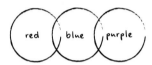

she came in like. . . . .like,

a crook only looking to break things, you see. . .

i left the front door open because i knew her,

very well i thought, but sometimes you can never tell,

friend or foe, heaven or hell. . .

who knows her motives, to what reason can anyone draw,

if anyone saw, it was me,

you see...and since i knew her,

i left the front door open. . .

i never questioned the door being left opened before,

but i did open my eyes,

and found this mask and familiar disguise.

her hand and another mans hand fleeing a crime scene,

you see,

i left the front door open,

and she broke everything, except the table,

she broke everything, except the tv,

she broke everything, except the cabinets, the windows, and
dresser. . . you see,

i left the front door open and she broke my heart. . .

which was everything.

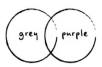

walk with me,

to the edge of things we don't understand,

where the universe can be,

whatever it needs to be...

while you and i,

walk.

grey

a beam of sun through a glass door,

explored the floor below me,

creating shades,

of black and greys-

that rehearse some calculated story....

equal in beauty,

perhaps by chance,

were the jealous clouds-

blocking with hands

that seemed to cover the world.

grey

i saw a homeless man,

mild in temper,

place his dreams inside a can....

he took that can -

(if i remember),

and placed it here with aching hands,

to be viewed by the many.....many people,

that will never care.

youth and i have been growing apart it seems...

dreams,

of forever,

rarely ever-

visit anymore,

instead, the inevitability of death,

the bully of good things,

accompanies my every step....

transforming my vein decisions,

into hope.

the world may never know,

this hold....

this......thing, you have over me,

which easily traps me....puzzles me,

keeps me here....close,

in your small room, with the smell of scrambled eggs crawling
down the hallway –

questioning my visit....perplexed at my stay,

the wind joins in conversation throwing whispers my way,

through cracked windows that gentle hands

(such as yours)

could unknowingly plan this way...during all of this,

during this short slice of time –

where smells and fragrances and whispers caught in the wind
question me,

(thoughts the universe pour into my simple mind)

your smile appears in the hallway entrance,

and i realize,

you are worth all the roses....

you are worth every risk.

grey

when you really wanna write,

sometimes,

you shouldn't write a thing,

because,

all beautiful things weren't meant–

to recite,

some were meant to live

outside the edges of memory.

purple

i'm not really sure,

why i'm so sure,

this is a sure thing.....

but for what it's worth,

trust me.

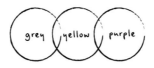

grey yellow purple

my life in my suitcase,

my thoughts in my coffee cup,

my heart in my palm,

which closes perfectly around her palm,

and in-between our skin,

lies the entire universe.

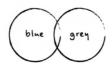

while a small child laughs in the distance,

imagining things they'll never remember,

i remain silent...

writing poems,

about things that use to matter,

long ago.

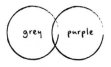

sometimes i wonder,

if your eyes could speak...

when ours meet,

would they speak the same language?

dangerous,

i know–

because my positions a float,

and the recent storm caused my ship to drift–

far from its anchored coast,

and still....

through the storm,

your eyes seem to calm me,

in some way i've yet to learn.

we began this life,

our life,

near the shore....

i adore the things that make you....you.

complicated,

but the taste i once tasted,

which had flavor,

is now the very thing bland to me,

i fought against the natural things to stay with you,

like a small ship fights the drifting effect,

or a wave,

(regardless)

all i have really are the words on this page,

and a hidden away cave,

very remote,

i retreat to when it rains this hard.

I am more alive now,

in this very moment,

then i've ever been in my teeny-tiny life,

which is why i write,

in hopes that

these prayer like poems,

can be answered

through a multitude of moments,

just like this one.

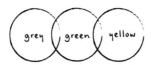

i woke up,

kidnapped, to my disbelief...

cramped in some small trunk,

finding a hole, i took a peak,

and i realized,

my dream had taken me captive.

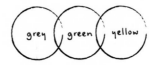

i saw a rose and i suppose,

this rose will come to die,

for now its june, the whether soon,

will grip and take its life...

but then again i may be wrong,

i have been wrong before,

i'll let the wind howl its song,

and seasons play their chord, (sigh)..

all the seasons thrown our way.....

winters coldest touch,

the rose from june is here today,

the leaves have all gave up,

i guess i was wrong, after all,

i have been wrong before...

as words drip from paint brush tips

and stain a marble floor, we laugh,

i and the rose,

as we grow old together. . .

grey

the loudest sound known to man,

is not a room of clapping hands,

its not guitars in metal bands,

or the crashing clash of pots and pans......

.

the loudest sound known to man,

is the silent air between a glance,

for in this silence...

everything can be heard.

grey

the day tends to creep along,

with its arms,

and its knees,

crawling through time,

exhaling a breeze....or at times,

a tornado like sneeze,

like some allergy hard to explain,

either way...

however you say it,

today will end.

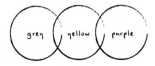

grey   yellow   purple

there are things unseen, that i've seen asleep,

the sound of snow, the humble feet-

of spiders crawling atop a peach,

smaller than the grains of sand,

that cloths the land along a beach,

the whispering wind, pretends to speak,

to draw me in, then kiss my cheek. . .

ohhh, how cold the lips of life can be,

the dying screams of falling leaves,

as tear drops fall from maple trees,

i've seen all this, these things unseen,

all these observed, only in dreams,

you though. . .

with your invisible qualities, that now i've seen,

makes me question . . . (is this a dream?)

or merely reflections of light,

bouncing off an ocean of personality,

that i, the sailor- never noticed, this unseen reality,

until the ocean and sun align, and my eyes are opened,

how beautiful it is, these things to be,

finally a dream,

i am awake to see. . .

grey

when the man with a guilty conscious,

walked into the room,

we assumed –

this afternoon,

was the worst he's ever had.....

no gift with balloons –

or some young lady that catches eyes

with her sweet lingering perfume –

could relieve the weight that lies,

just along the shoulders...near the top of his spine,

.... "would you like some coffee?" the waitress spoke,

"dark....please" as he reclined,

................we never had a full conversation,

although he asked me for the time,

his face told me enough,

his face told me enough.

i've never been more sure about something in my life.

its almost like seeing bright light

for the first time break through the clouds

while no ones around

and being sure this thing you see,

is anything but the sun.

it has to be, right?

i feel...

full, in the best of ways.

i've discovered a universal truth

that'll one day break through the clouds for you

like blue

through white,

or maybe it'll hit you in a more subtle way,

as it did me.

on a walk perhaps,

you'll stop....and take a second

to look down at your feet.

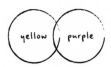

today.....

i looked for the sun,

......i mean,

her smile,

and like a child

that learns to run,

oh how happy i am in its discovery.

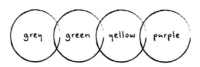

grey green yellow purple

"sit here....beside me."

i asked "why?" –

to no reply,

she grabbed my hand,

while our eyes followed the stars....

and God,

(if you believe),

would breath into our hearts,

a desire for wings......and things,

we've never seen.

grey

looking out the small window,

silent...

and completely still,

i feel the quiet,

and gentle hands of time...

peel away my worries.

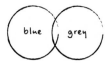

there comes a time,

you know,

when life drops a question at your feet....

and that problem....grows,

into the thoughts that wake you from your sleep.

there comes a time....

you know.

when the things you wish for....die,

the air that's too cold, blows....

the truth, that's so true....lies.

there's always time for many things,

.........there's never time for me.

43

do we really change?

or,

are we only making adjustments to the person we'll always be?

let me explain....

you see,

my soon to be,

became....

and the good changes i saw,

changed....

into something she use to be,

and i no longer recognized.

funny...

what she wanted me to become,

i strangely could never be,

i could try my best to adjust,

and compromise to whatever degree,

yet and still...

we tried our best.

we had our run.

a drifting, sleepy horizon....

rolls in the distance,

too far for hands,

it touches me,

and my plans....change,

from leaving, to watching silently,

the architect of this world,

paint.

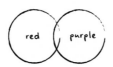

the distance,

between our eyes,

has grown....

and its shown,

through your lies,

and disguise you chose, makeup...

sometimes,

its too late for makeup

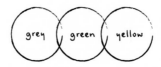

a fog.....or mist from my imagination,

somehow spilled onto the floor...

and whats more,

i and this shadow of dreams had a conversation,

about impossible things...

and big windows,

i love big windows....

purple

there are not enough days

- in a year,

to explain the things,

so near,

like a whisper,

in ear,

filled with things i cant understand....

(or you cant explain),

in either case,

in either place,

yours or mine,

im happy...and dumb.

grey / purple

ya know, theres still some things I've yet to tell you,

a couple of letters I've yet to mail you,

a couple of moments i felt like fell through,

simply because,

i couldn't say.... "i love you".

i feel it...i do,

so why couldn't i tell you?

did society make me believe more time should pass,

before that thought could reach the heart,

from reach to grasp?

I've grown tired of peoples opinions i guess.

i got it!

i got it...lets walk to the edge of our minds together,

better yet,

lets watch the universe spin out of control near the soles of our shoes,

me and you......

you and i.

in love.

grey

death wears a disguise,

and trails us distantly in youth,

as not to alarm us...in surprise,

but sometimes...

oddly enough,

death,

reserves us a seat...

just inside your peripheral,

and yet,

just beyond your reach,

where whispers are mistaken as wind,

between arriving.....and leaving.....

we live.

i can drift into a lot of nothing with you,

anything really with you.....is good,

as long as, well,

you know,

you continue to blossom....

and i.......

..........i'll show the qualities you search for,

in a man.

grey

sometimes,

if by chance...your silent enough,

and find the time,

to find the time,

you've already lost....

i hope in your finding it,

you smile,

realizing how small we all are,

as you fade into the unknown,

or whatever it is you believe comes after death.

being human,

being lost,

chasing dreams

across the sky,

at what cost

do we chase?

how long should we try?

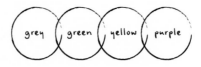

im not sure who you are.....

really,

i dont know you....

but i feel like i do.....

silly,

to think our lives are mapped out,

or written on the skies hand,

when plans.....as you know,

look clearer further away.

knowing this,

knowing this...

i take the risk, and say............ "hi"

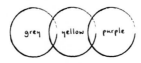

can you hear it?

the crashing waves...

rolling over and under itself,

while i pen the page,

over and under our hearts...

in cursive....engraved,

over and under, and over again.

grey

i know i dream....i know,

but i always forget them though....

where do they hide when we wake?

how do they come and go?

memories i suppose.....are like dreams,

or wildly painted scenes,

that draw near the things forgotten....sometimes,

well....most times,

they'll never see the surface,

but fade where their birth is -

in some dark place,

you'll see and forget when you wake.

grey

the edge of the tree line, in my mind,

is lined with maple trees (i believe),

and the leaves (if green), are the moments i've seen,

that are now memories for me,

as for the orange and reds,

and leaves that start to fade,

these are memories much further than yesterday,

.....would you not agree?

that the oranges and reds are the prettiest to see,

the golden moments from long ago....that we know,

we'll never live again.

and

of course,

as age creeps in,

even those vivid colors we saw,

those memories with so much detail will turn brown and fall...

possibly raked up from time to time,

near the distant parts of our mind, where names are forgotten,

and faces look the same.

there is a world that separates us,

oceans lie between the very ideas,

and yet....

you appear.....in dreams i've never had,

even with this distance, i've never felt closer to anything in
my life.

bored with not knowing,

tired of mights.....maybes....

nights where the crazy,

and logical thoughts,

merge in my mind,

becoming one big question,

that time.....and fools can answer.

(sigh) however they reply,

whenever this answer falls across my pillow,

i wonder if i.....upon asking,

can be relieved of this weight....that probably doesnt exist.

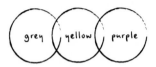

grey yellow purple

there's something in her eyes....

im not quite sure what it is,

but their depth entangles me......every time.

their silence, is too loud for quiet places,

trapping me with every breath....to leave....to stay....

to leave....to stay....

leave.

stay.

grey

drifting in and out of consciousness,

sleepy....

but not sleep,

i reach for the cool darkness,

trying to persuade relief,

to push against my eyelids,

and pull out the key,

that opens the door of dreams,

hidden behind sheets,

and many trivial things,

that keep me awake.

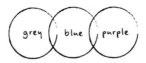

grey   blue   purple

although we've never met in this life,

i feel like we have in times before....is this strange?

maybe we were best friends in Sicily circa 1472,

perhaps we dreamed

of future times, future things,

settling back in the chair my mother owned,

i ask myself, by myself....old, and alone,

if i made the wrong decision....had i been the fool?

there are things we'll never learn or understand in this life,

my life...only being to have your heart near mine.

if you would ever notice...

i would easily let you have everything and anything,

even the moons light

(that shines bright on people in love)

even that....since its no matter to me,

for that light is one i haven't seen in quite some time.

rhymes.....lines.....metaphors....love,

who cares? besides i....

who cares?

besides us.....who cares?

i met a traveling man today,

who spoke of everything and nothing,

i asked'em, "how long ya here to stay?"

"my whole life if im lucky."

"lucky? how so?" i replied,

his response broken only by the lady near his side,

whose eyes caught his,

and paused his speech...and mine,

almost as if a sign,

some invisible confirmation was given between the two,

that no one else on the entire train knew,

except them, we all were cold...

except them.

grey

these thoughts i have,

the things racing around my mind,

i wish i could pour them into a glass,

or flask,

and share them with you all....one at a time,

we take shots of things hard to comprehend.

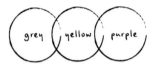

you are like my favorite tea,

the imported kind...from some far away place,

steeped in beauty and culture,

with a taste,

only my palette can recognize,

and the kind of depth minds get lost in.

minds such as mine,

i've grown sick of water all the time,

whats a heart without you?

whats a mug without my favorite tea?

she is willing to give me everything,

this i can see,

time, love, whatever it maybe,

the very thing i want however;

is floating in the eyes,

its that same thing you see during any sunrise,

when you stare between earth and sky,

and ponder how they've been able to hold hands for so long....

it's the magic a mother can only pass down,

which grows into something special,

although she's special,

and the coolest in all sense,

she still has no idea how to step between shadows,

she cant capture unicorns with her whisper,

only men,

because....again,

she's great!

just not what im looking for.

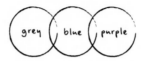

grey   blue   purple

yesterday morning....October 10th,

i helped carry my grandmother to her grave site,

my hand on the casket rail,

we lift with a sigh'

(heavy)

despite -

her lightweight appearance in life, (85 pounds)

we wondered,

"how can a small women be this heavy inside?",

the casket was sleek....grey....light weight -

until her light frame was laid inside,

puzzling....how the weight of this women could weigh on my
mind,

it wasn't until the ride home,

and stories told on the way,

that i realized the weight of that women, that day.

(heavy)

[R.I.P. Betty McGee....wish i took more time, to get to know
you, when you were alive]

i remember being little,

asking my dad,

"what do we call this sound?"

with a smile,

and a lift of his brow,

he replied,

".......jazz",

but many years passed......

many years passed,

since i've heard that melody again,

until a cold night in Georgia,

at some restaurant i've never seen,

i was once again acquainted with melodies from younger
dreams,

by chance (if there is such a thing),

a friend asked,

(while peering into the glass)

"wow...whats the name?"

with a smile and a lift of my brow,

i replied,

".......jazz."

the next page gives a brief description of
what the colors represent above
the poems....
each color being the mood i was in while writing.

moods
(written while....)

red
frustrated, upset, or extremely passionate.

blue
sad, down, or not really passionate about anything.

grey
reflective, trying to understand whatever the
universe lays before me.

green
curious, looking over the hill, adventurous mind-set.

yellow
very happy, a sense of euphoria.

purple
someone was on my mind, whether I knew them or
not.

the

~~end~~

beginning.

pages 80 - 114

(grey thoughts and blank pages)

For the last 3 years I've been conducting
poetry workshops with a crew of creatives, writers,
homeless folks, athletes (really diverse groups)
in the community.

Each session we have always consisted of
exercises I'll put together or with the help of the
group, collectively come up with.

The point of these exercises were intended to not
only experience something amazing together, but
to also work out different parts of the creative self.

Whether you write, draw, play sports, engineer,
whatever it is, we all felt that exercising this
creative muscle in various ways, once you applied
it to your own particular craft, could add a
beautiful texture toward everything you do.
With that said, I hope you enjoy the moments
created from pages 80 onward.

go for a nice 30 minute walk...wherever you end up after
the walk, write a poem from the perspective of your shoes.
how they felt during and after the walk, what they saw,
can they even see? or smell?

think of someone you love, that does not live with you....
after that, write a poem that has a theme around their
small almost invisible quality that only few may even
recognize.
for example: bill withers wrote a song not about his
grandmothers great cooking, or beautiful eyes / smile....
he wrote a song about his grandma's hands.
even ending the song with "when i get to heaven, i'll look
for grandma's hands". those hands symbolized strength,
wisdom, tenderness, discipline, and love. a lot of times,
the small things we see in people is what makes
the love so much bigger.

once you have something completed...go ahead and mail
your poem to them. you can put it on a greeting card,
a napkin, rip it from the blank pages of this book,
whatever....just let it be hand written. even if you have
the worst handwriting in the world. let the reader feel in
every sense of the word, what you were trying to say.

you have 5 minutes to write a poem that must include these three words:
shadows, the entire title of a song you really like, and the last word from the last text message or email someone sent you.

find a homeless or less fortunate person than yourself and
donate a little of your time or resources to their situation.
be in the moment with them.
have an exchange of energy and see yourself for a second....
your own reflection in their face. what's their name?
where are they from? how do they see the world? after
awhile, leave....go to your writing space, whatever that looks
like, and write. you don't have to write a poem or journal....
try to write a color. push the feeling and emotion of the
moment and situation into your fingers,
then into words on paper. whenever you can tap into that
wholeness, it'll almost feel like a prayer you've written....
and whats more, whose to say it isn't?

go to youtube and search "erik satie - gymnopedie no.1"
and write until its finished playing.
which gives you a little over 3 minutes maybe.

text or ask a friend to give you three random words.
whatever these random words are, you must write a poem
the same day using the words.
add difficulty by timing this, like 10 minutes to complete,
then next time 5 minutes, then maybe 3 minutes...
in our collective we push at 30 seconds sometimes, share
what we have so far, then finish on 2 minutes.

here is your theme: you were caught in a different country
and charged for something you are innocent of.
regardless of this, you are given a pen and paper and have
15 minutes to write. after this, you will be executed.
place yourself there mentally....now write.

here is your theme: everything you've ever dreamed of,
is coming true. it hasn't quite happened yet,
but everything is lining up and looking better than its ever
looked before. your excited!
the complicated part of it all, because in life its always
something lol, it involves you breaking up with someone.
i mean you really care about the person deeply,
you think you might even love them maybe.
but the idea of leaving that "person" is looking a lot
healthier and better than staying.

you have 5 minutes to complete this poem.

here is your theme: you were just caught doing something
you are completely ashamed of.
your embarrassed to the fullest degree.
you may or may not ever be forgiven for whatever it is
you've done.....place yourself there....
in this lowly place.
what color do you feel?
whatever emotion you see, really let it sit with you.
lay with it for a moment. embrace it. now write.

write something that tells an entire story in 6 words or less.
for example: legend has it, that ernest hemingway once
won a bet by writing a six word story,
"for sale: baby shoes. never worn."
now it's really difficult to prove whether the legend is true
or not....in either case, its still a great exercise.
you have 10 minutes
to write a few stories in 6 words or less...go!

write a poem that includes these 5 words:
essential, frontier, window, lost, and restroom.
if you search youtube:
"arcade fire - her photograph on a beach"
you'll see a song thats about 6 minutes and 1 second.
thats how much time you have to complete the poem....
start soon as the song starts.

words in grey

words in grey

words in grey

words in grey

words in grey

words in grey

words in grey

words in grey

words in grey

words in grey

words in grey

words in grey

words in grey

words in grey

words in grey

words in grey

words in grey

words in grey

words in grey

words in grey

words in grey

words in grey

words in grey

words in grey

. . . .

There were 12 soldiers marching by,
Each ate an apple off the tree,
and left 11

(they did not share, or clone the apple...
Each ate an entire apple and still left 11)

How?

. . . .

CPSIA information can be obtained
at www.ICGtesting.com
Printed in the USA
LVOW12s1437211216
518279LV00001B/130/P